Massive Bombshell

A 100% statistical correlation and scientific explanation for why the planet Mars can trigger stock market crashes. This pamphlet lays out the 25 major stock market crashes and downturns in US history. The data shows a 100% correlation between such events and Mars position in relation to the Earth

Anthony of Boston

© Copyright 2024 Anthony Moore

All Right Reserved

A 100% statistical correlation and scientific explanation for why the planet Mars can trigger stock market crashes. by Anthony of Boston

This paper lays out the 25 major stock market crashes and downturns in US history. The data shows a 100% correlation between such events and Mars position in relation to earth. Every stock market crash and major stock downturn in US history has happened when Mars was orbiting behind the sun from earth's point of view.

To gain relevant context in regards to what this paper is demonstraing, it is important to take into account a recent study published in Nature Communications in March of 2024, roughly 5 years after this idea was first introduced to the public. In that study published in March of 2024, researchers discovered that Mars is exerting a gravitation pull on earth's tilt, exposing earth to warmer temperatures and more sunlight, all within a 2.4 million year cycle. I assert that this allows us to surmise that, even within smaller timeframes, Mars is still exerting a gravitational pull on earth's axial tilt, enough to raise temperatures when the planet is within 30 degrees of the lunar node, which would affect human behavior. Citing the fact of numerous studies that link aggression and irritability to warmer temperatures, I establish an axiom and then assert that Mars within 30 degrees of the lunar node should affect the brain by reducing cognition and compelling aggression and irritability.

Here is a visual of what is happening as Mars travels around the sun and exerts a gravitational pull on Earth axial tilt. In this first graphic, Mars gravity is pulling earth's tilt away from the sun.

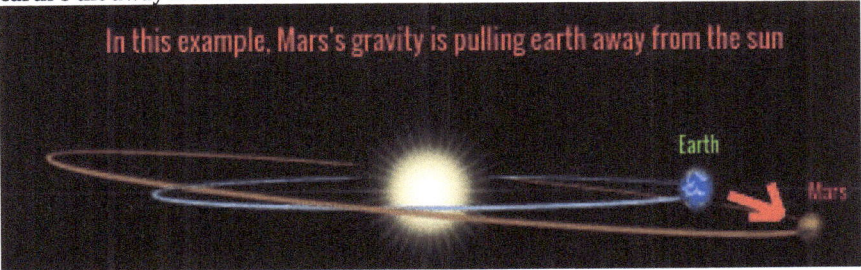

In this next graphic, Mars's gravity is pulling Earth's tilt toward the sun.

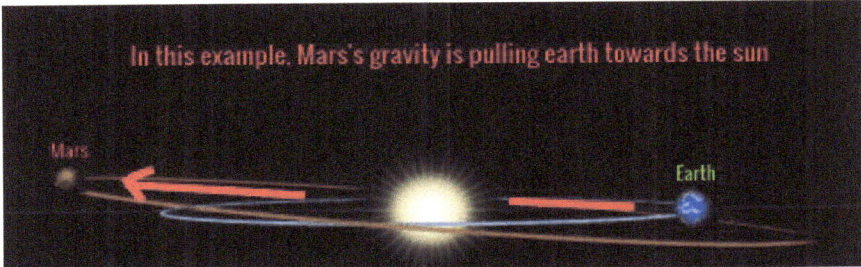

In this latter visual, this scenario should have the most prominent effect on human behavior. Here is how this scenario of Mars pulling earth's tilt towards the sun

appears in an astrology chart. This is the chart for the October 29, 1929 Stock market crash. Planet earth is always opposite the sun in an astrology chart.

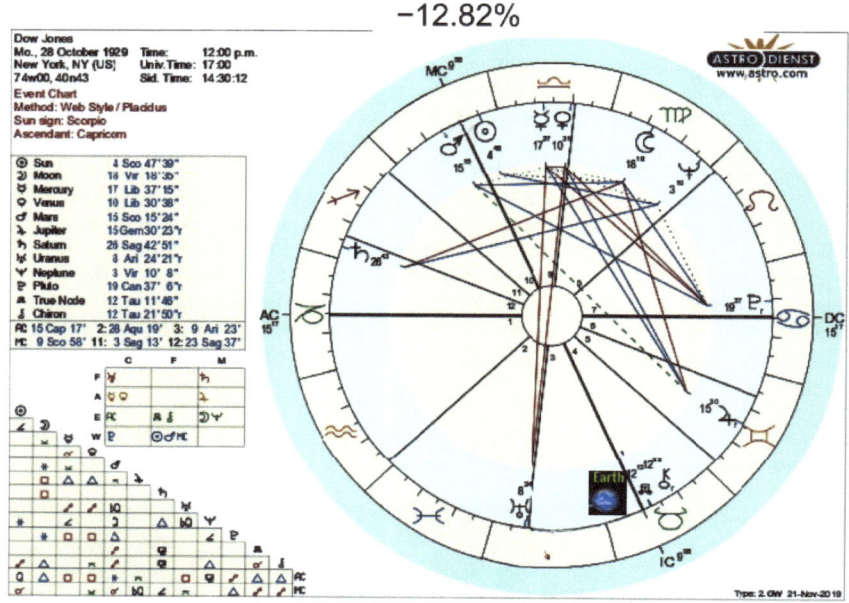

Here is the view from above of the same planetary configuration scenario.

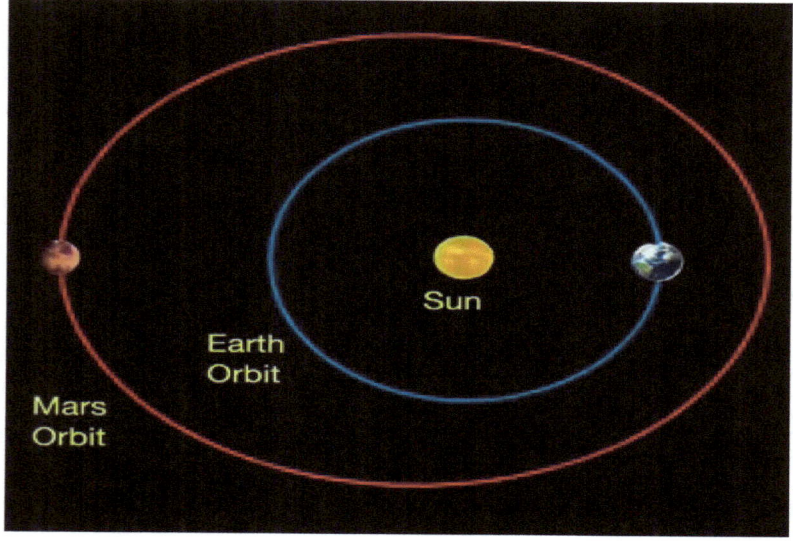

In all the major stock market crashes and one-day drops, Mars was somewhere along the white line as shown in this graphic, which according to the research, would indicate that Mars is pulling the earth's tilt towards the sun, triggering irritability

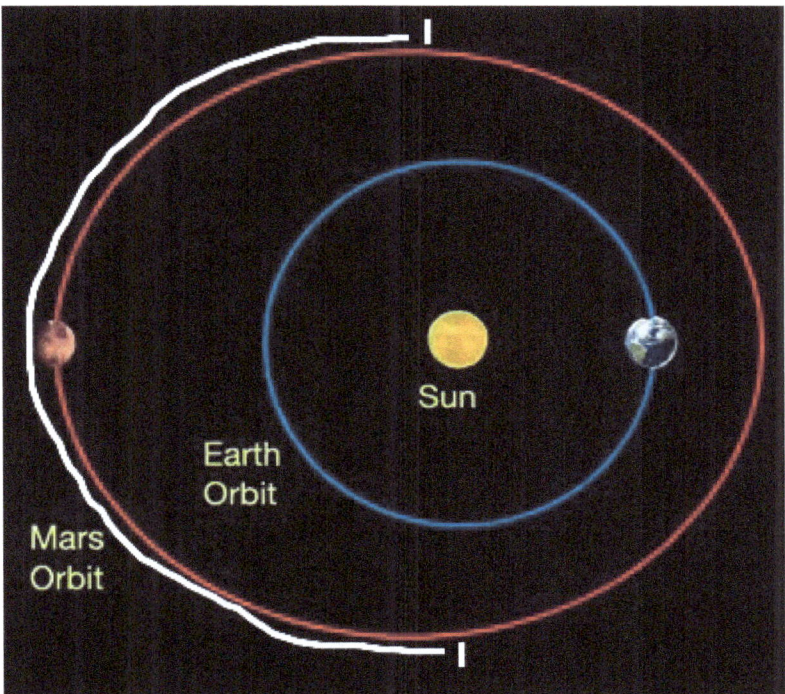

Here is how this same visual is represented in an astrology chart. See the next page Notice the white line.

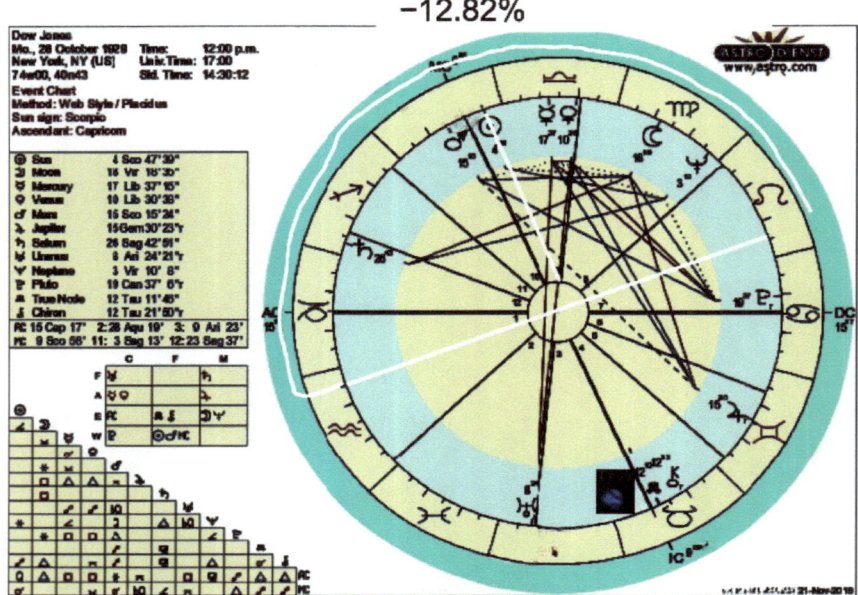

All the highest one day stock market crashes or one-day drops occurred when Mars appeared within that white line, as drawn out from the degree of the sun.

This perspective should help the reader move beyond the preconceived notion of absurdity and realize that this has scientific merit

Here are the rest of the stock market crashes, along with the astrology charts and the representation of Mars position in space

October 19, 1987 Stock market crash

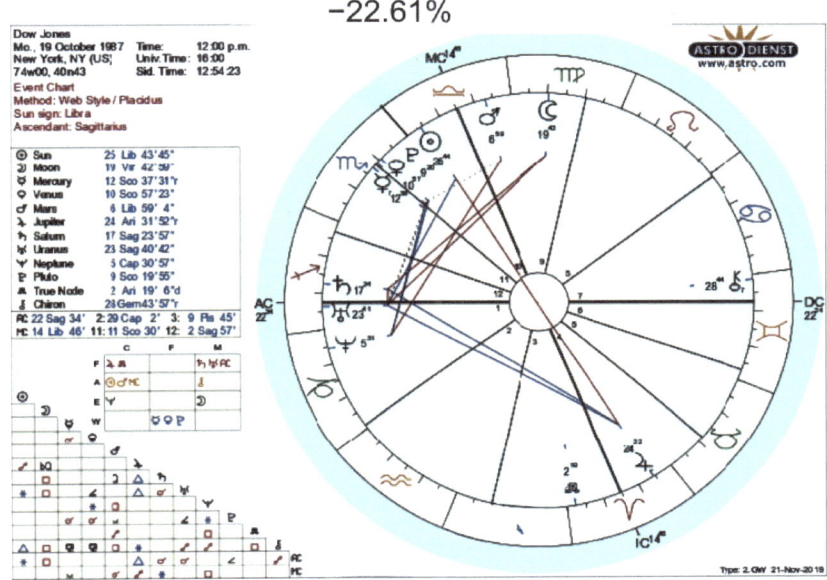

Here is how Mars was positioned in space that day relative to earth

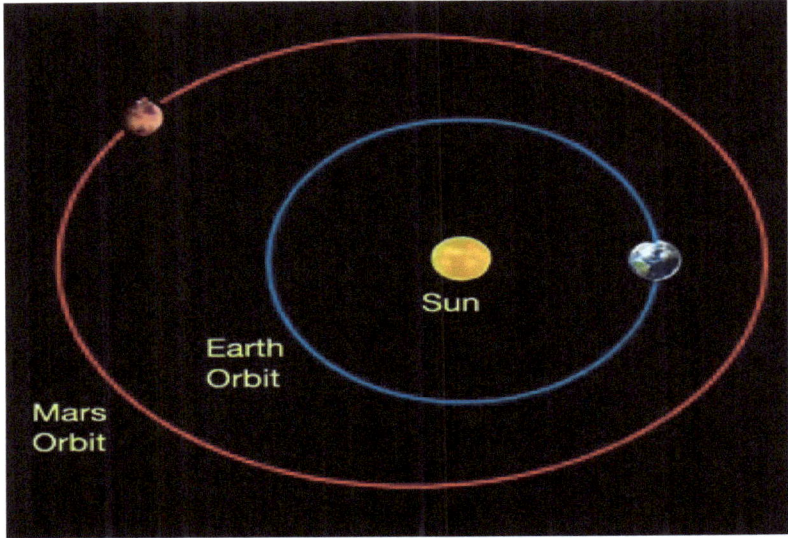

November 6 1929 Stock Market Crash

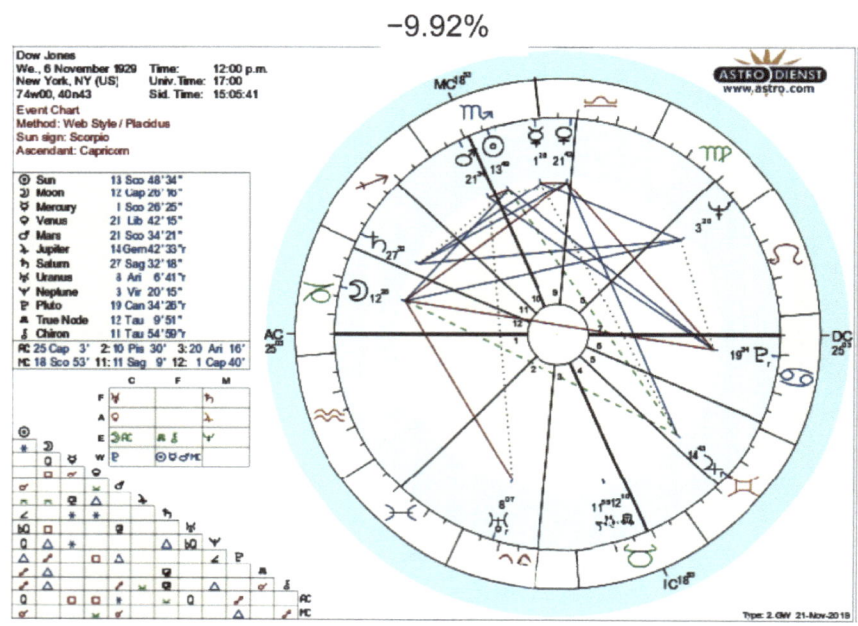

Here is where Mars was located in space from earth's point of view

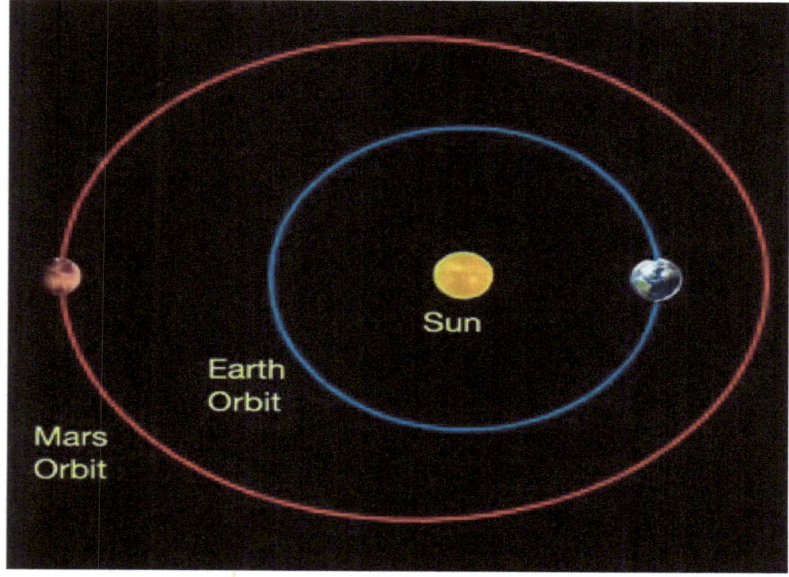

March 16, 2020 Stock Market crash

-12.93

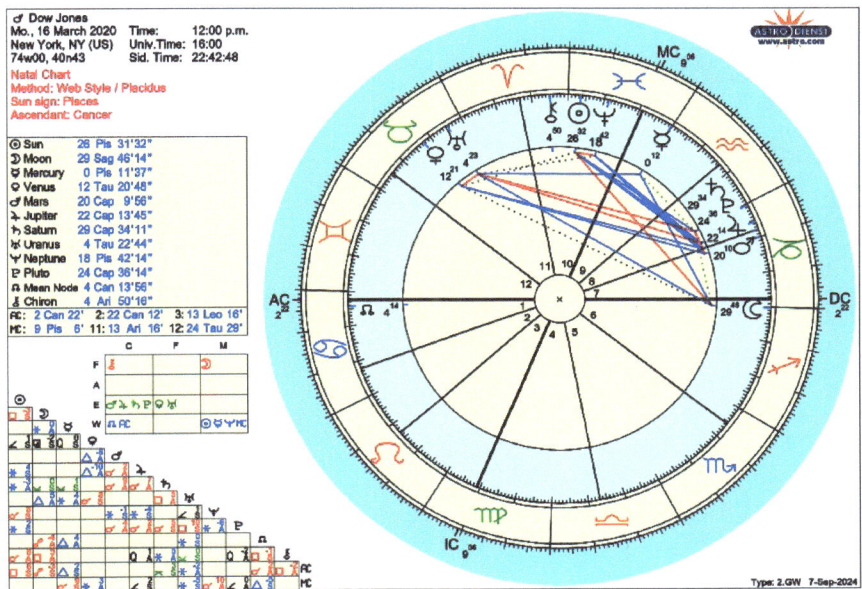

Here is how Mars was positioned in the sky relative to earth

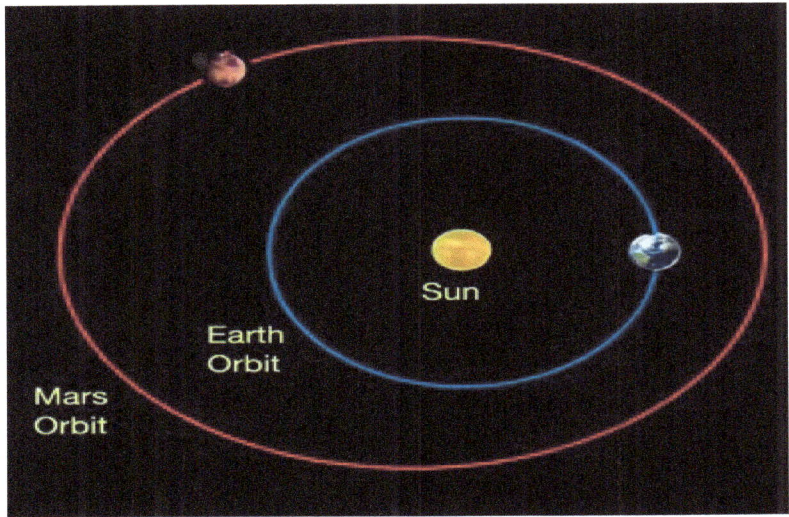

March 12, 2020 Stock Market Crash

-9.99

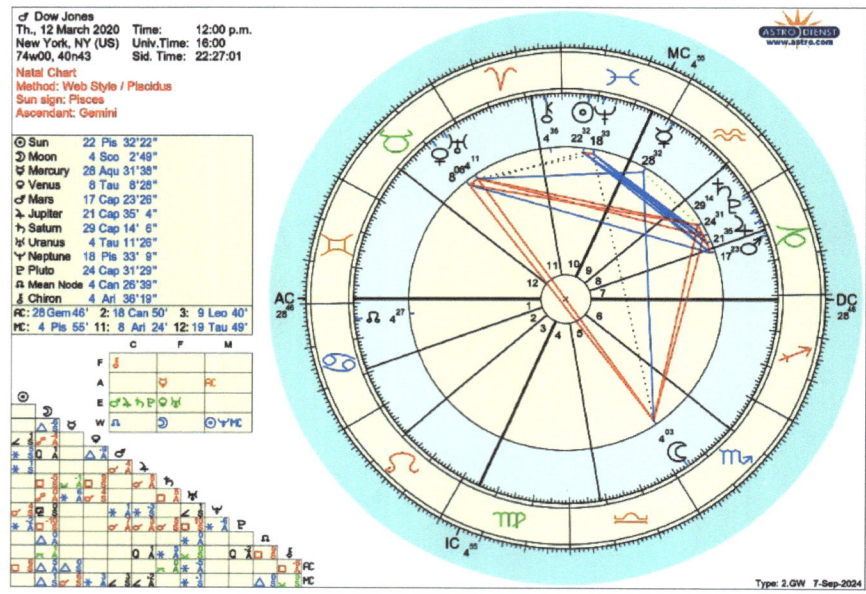

Here is how Mars was positioned in the sky on that day

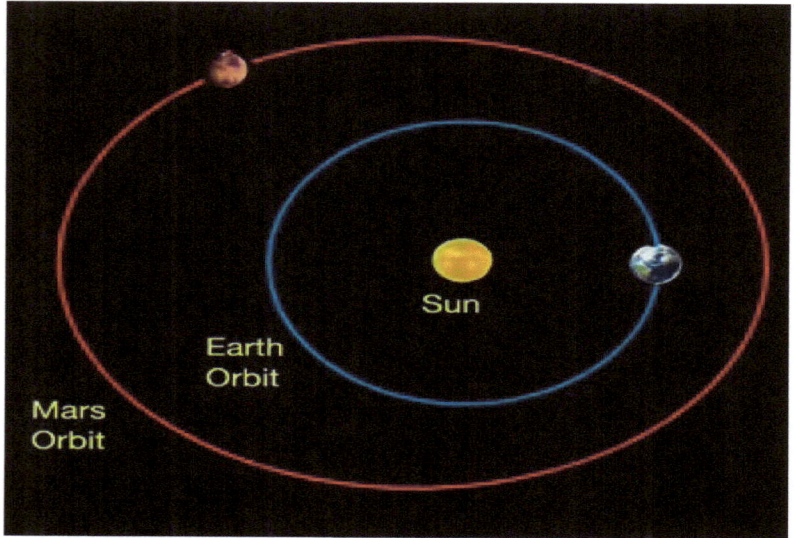

March 9, 2020 Stock Market Crash

-7.79

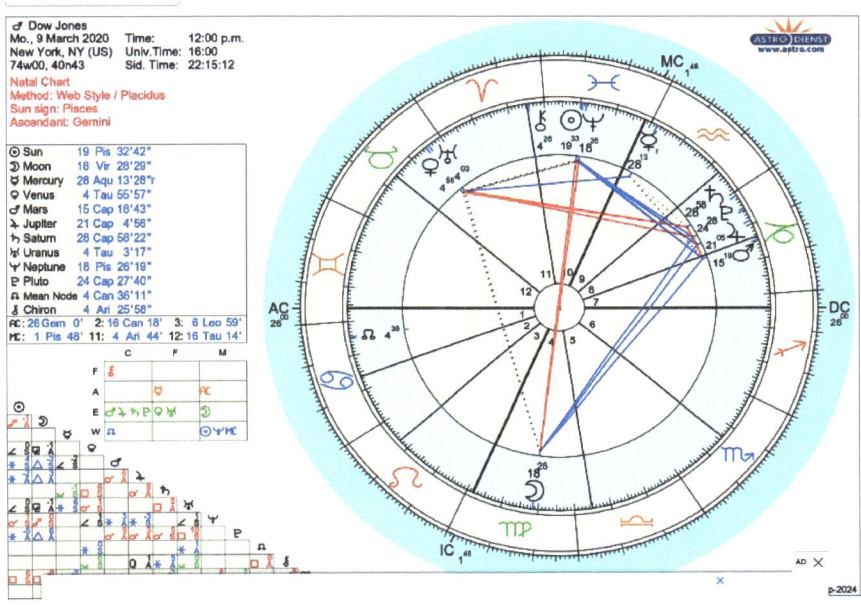

Here is where Mars was in the sky that day

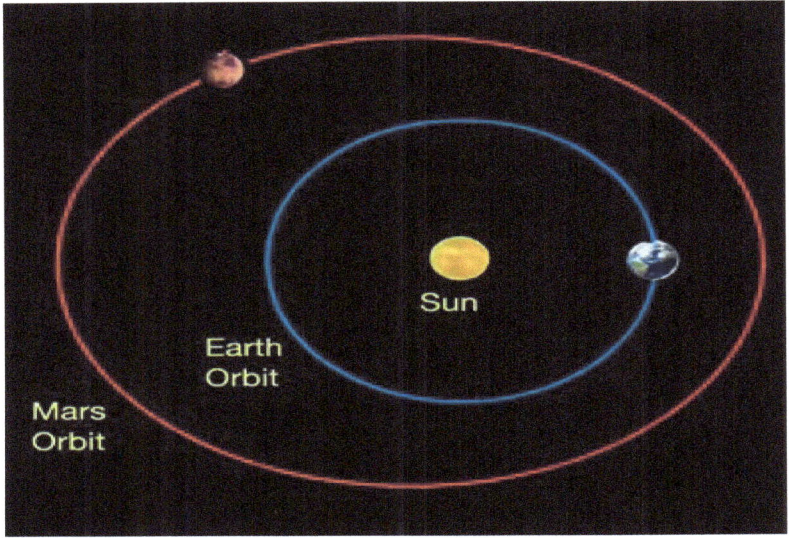

December 18, 1899, the stock market dropped -8.72 percent

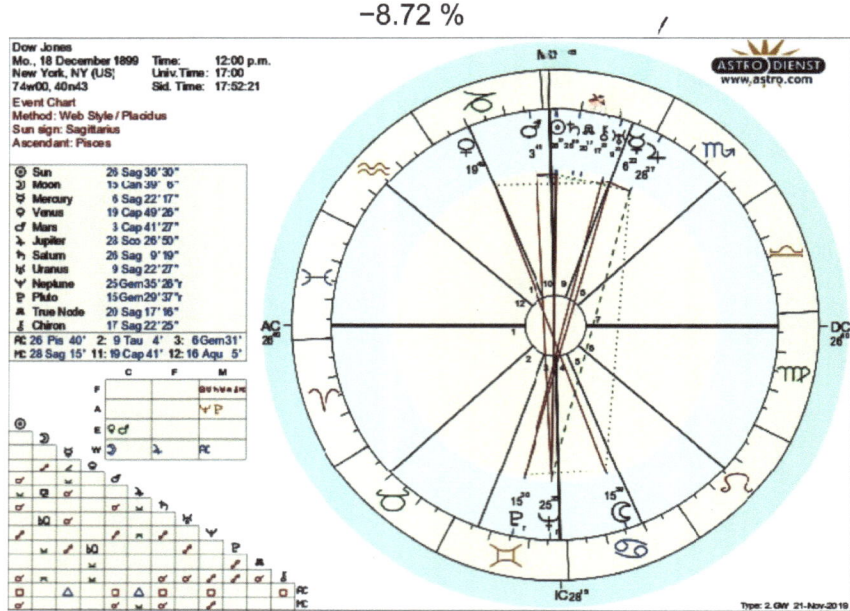

Here is how Mars lined up in the sky that day

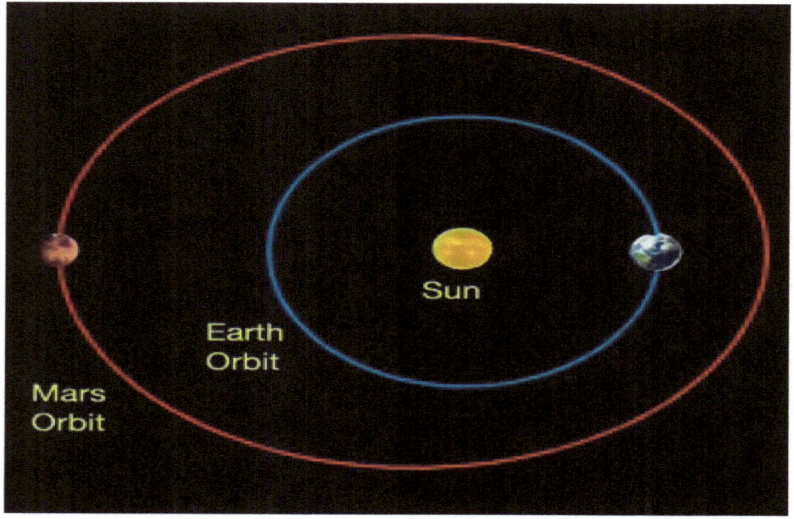

August 12, 1932, stock market dropped -8.4 %

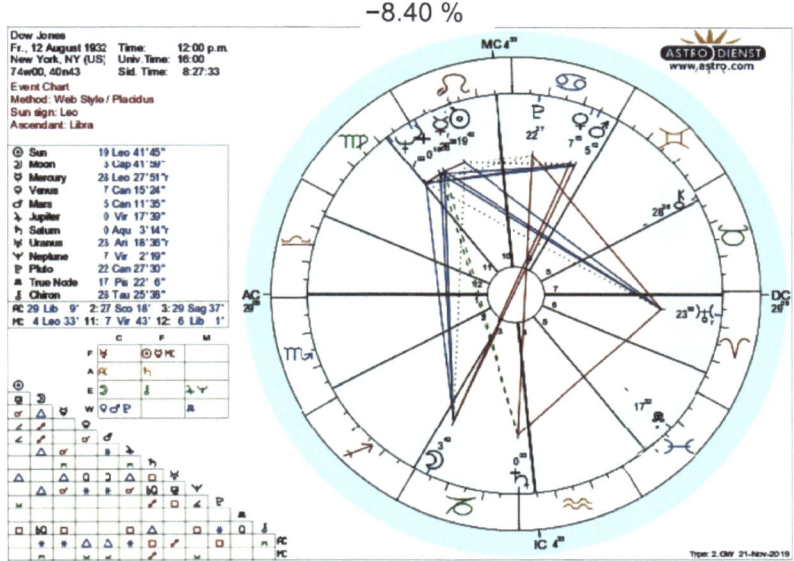

Here is how Mars was positioned in the sky that day

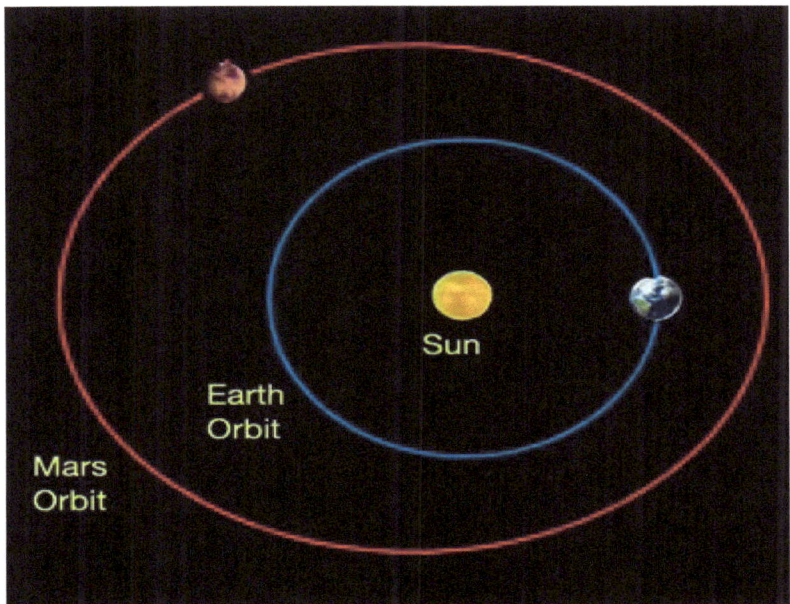

March 14, 1907, the stock market fell -8.29%

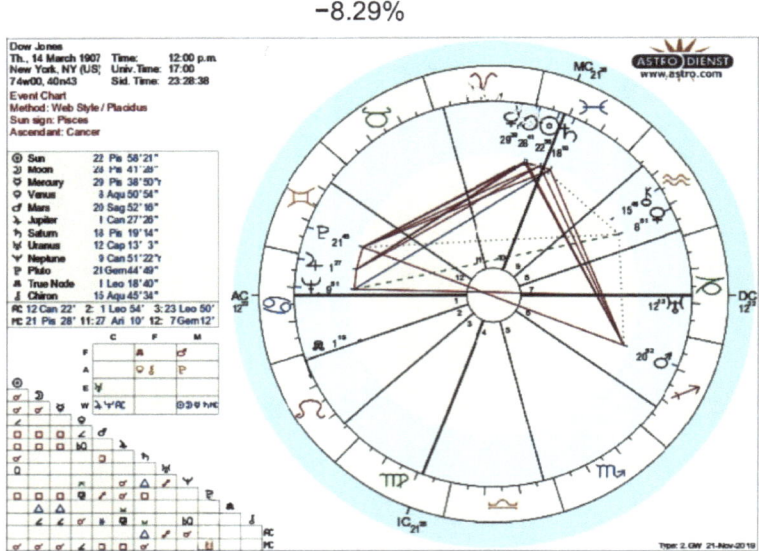

Here is how Mars was positioned in the sky that day

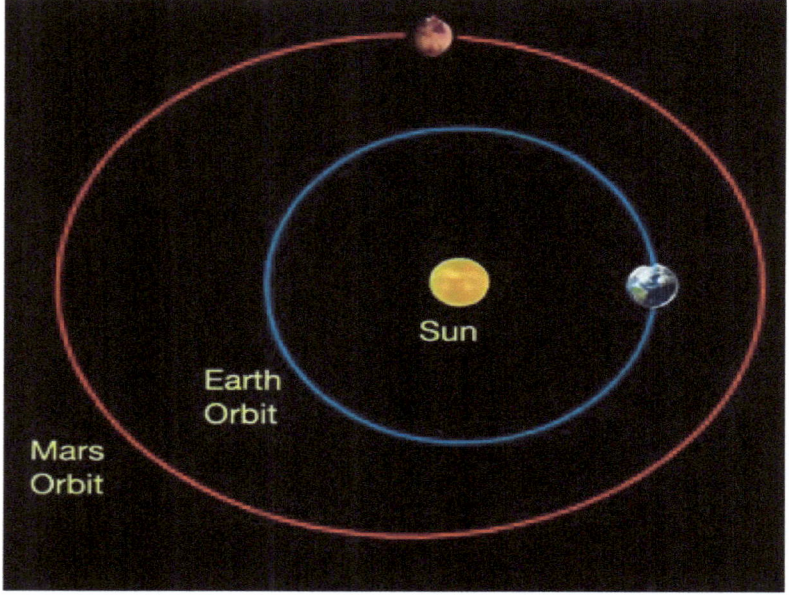

October 26, 1987, the stock market dropped -8.04%

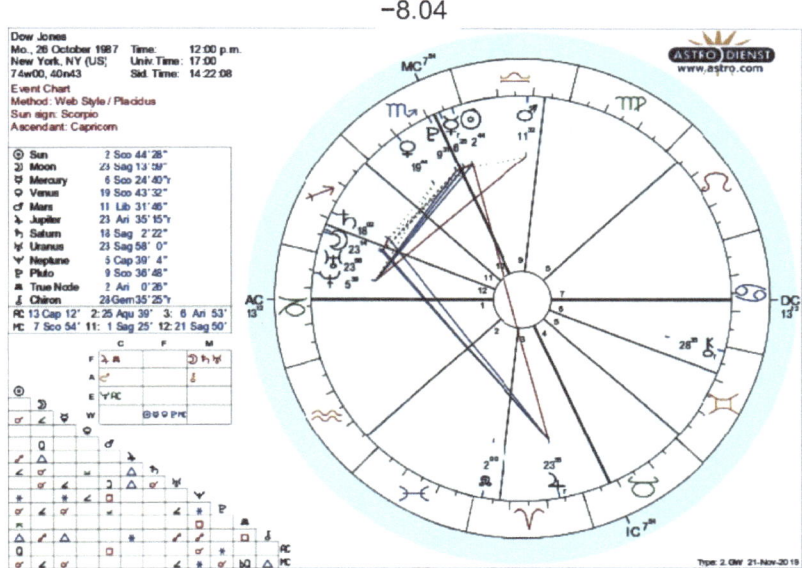

Here is where Mars was positioned in the sky that day

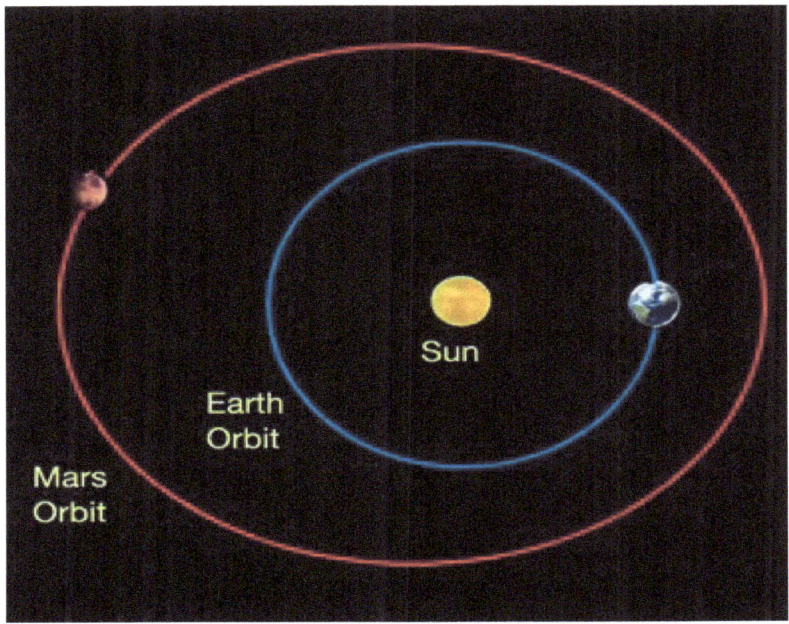

October 15, 2008, the stock market fell -7.87%

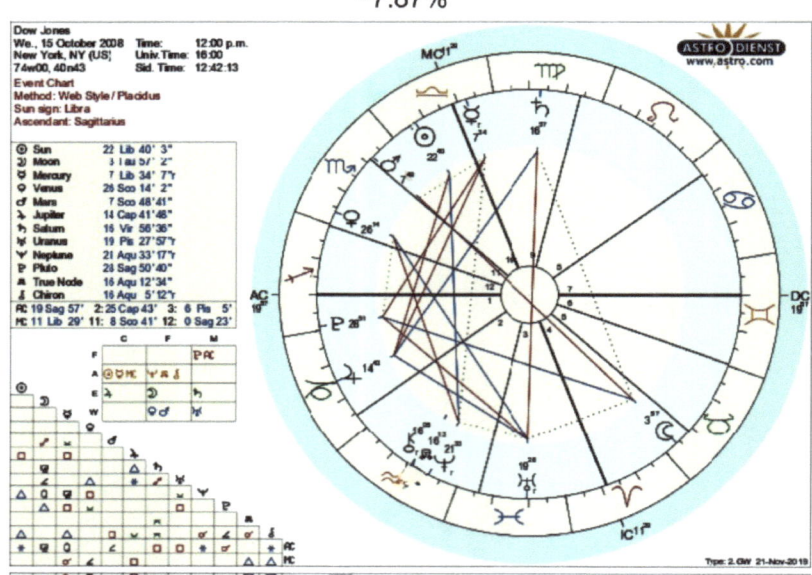

Here is where Mars was positioned in the sky that day

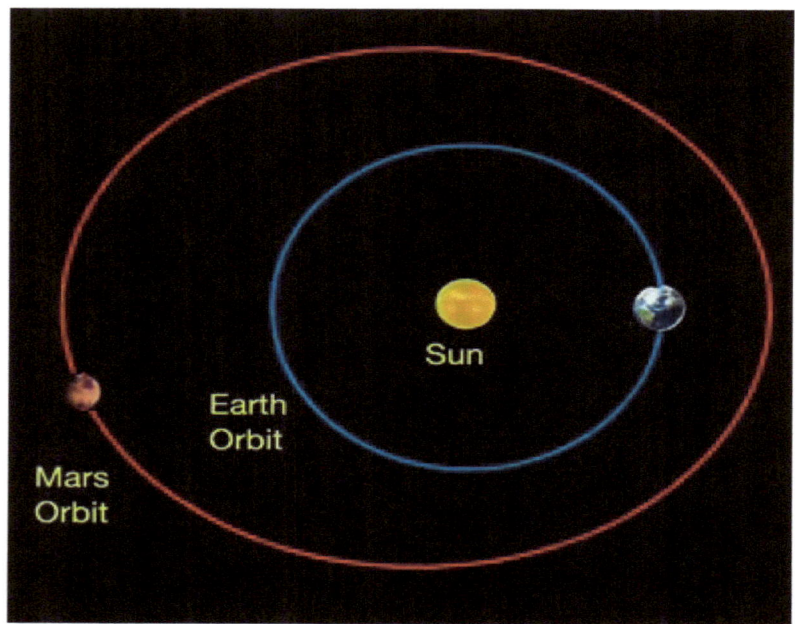

July 21, 1993, The stock market dropped -7.84

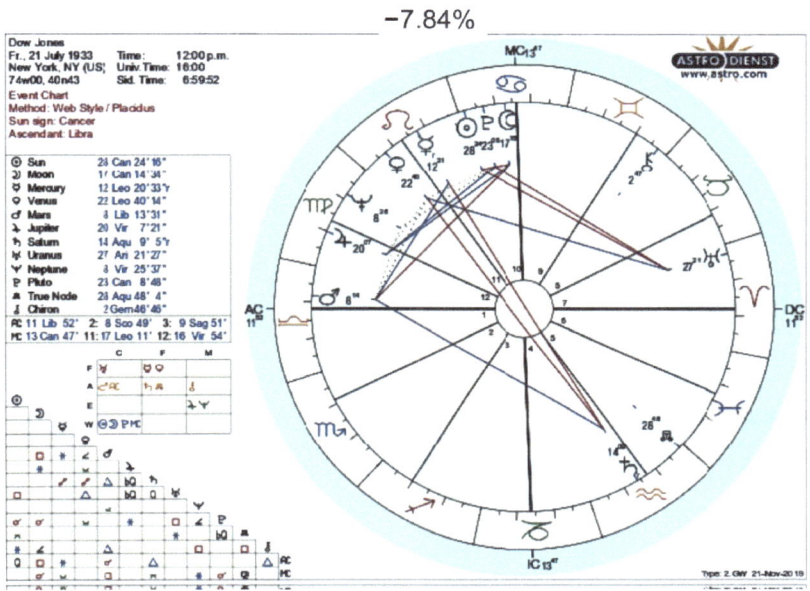

Here is where Mars was positioned in the sky that day

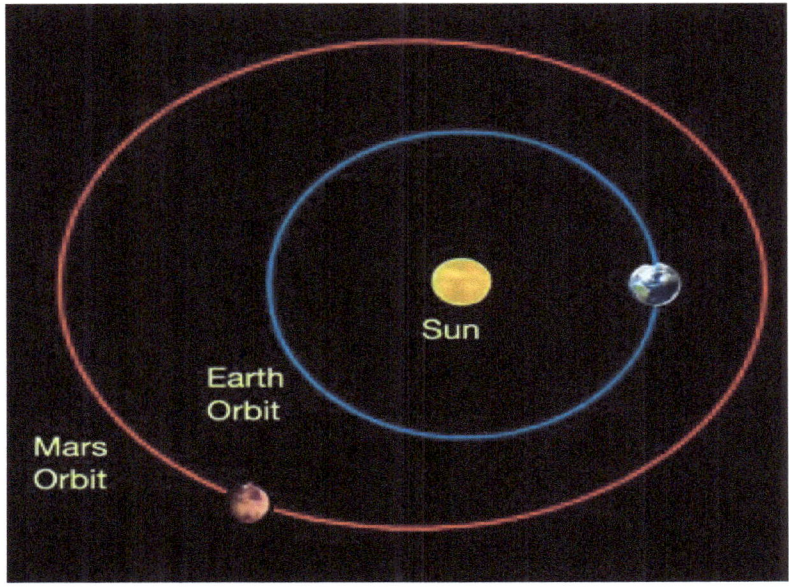

October 18, 1937, the stock market dropped -7.75%

−7.75%

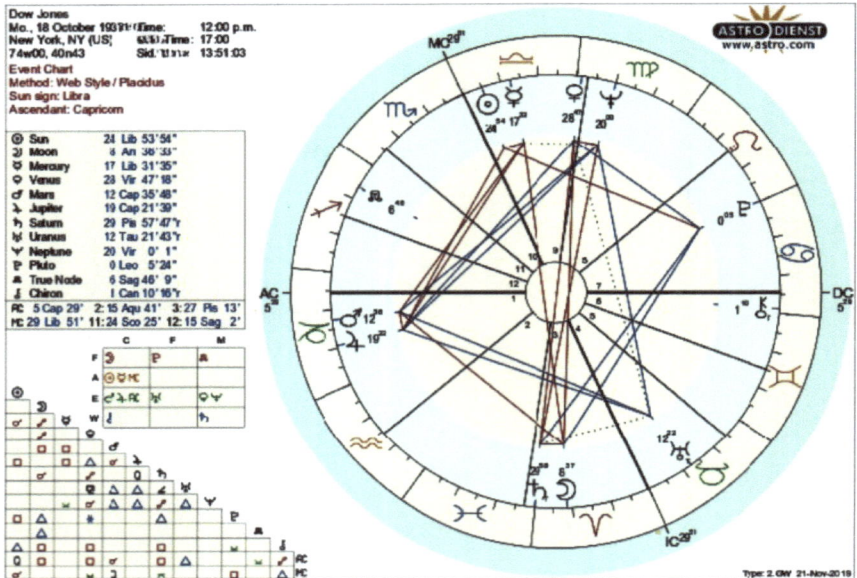

Here is where Mars was positioned on that day

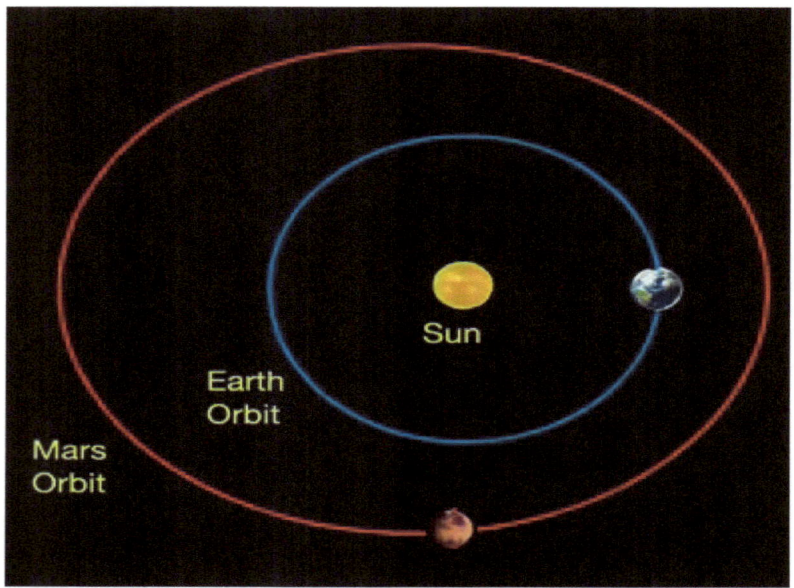

On December 1, 2008, the stock market dropped -7.70%

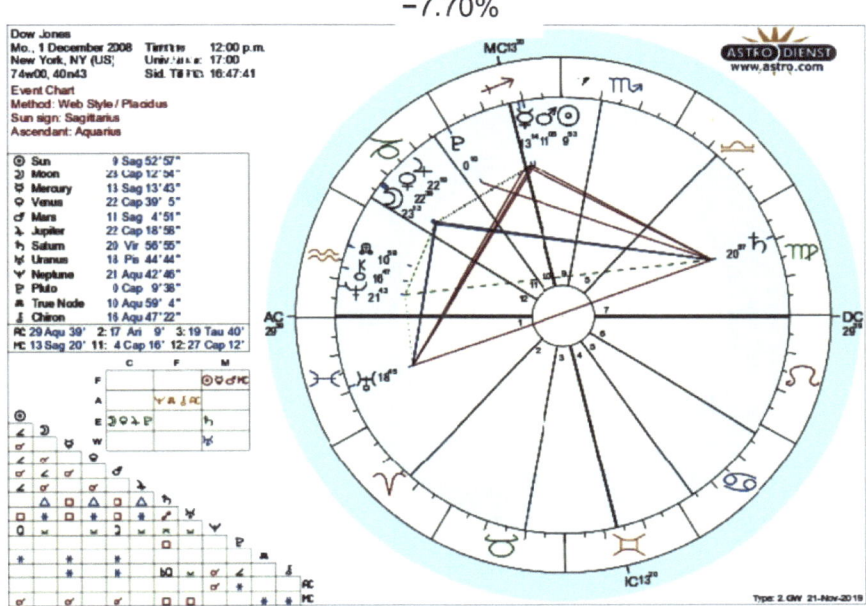

Here is where Mars was positioned in that sky that day

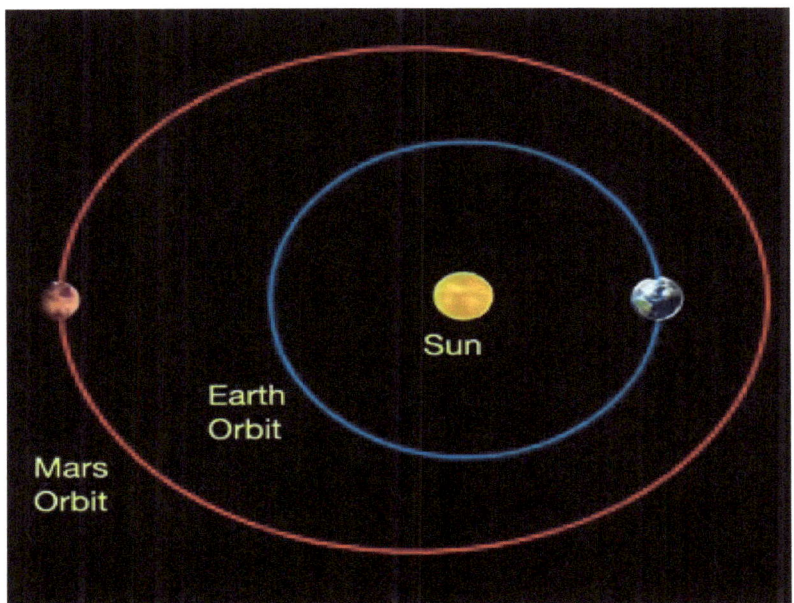

October 9, 2008, the stock market fell -7.33%

−7.33 %

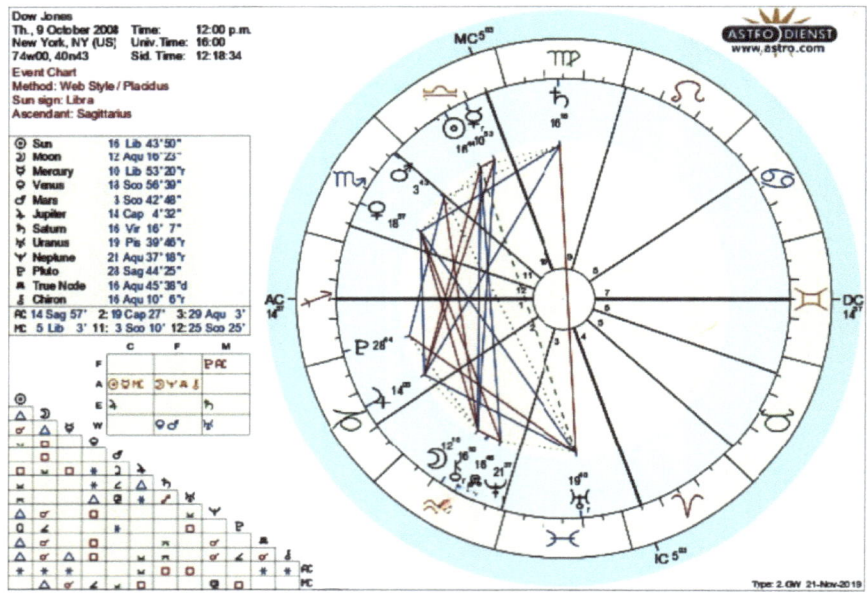

Here is where mars was positioned in the sky on that day

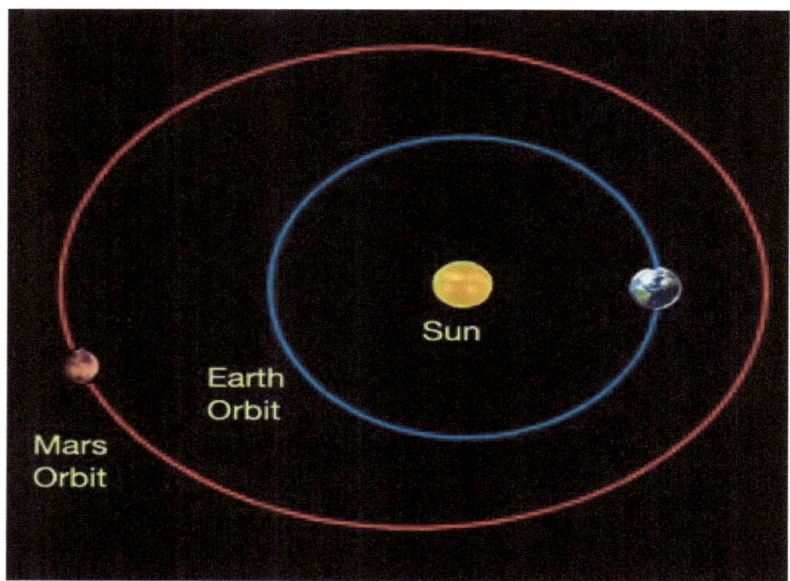

On February 1, 1917, the stock market dropped -7.24%

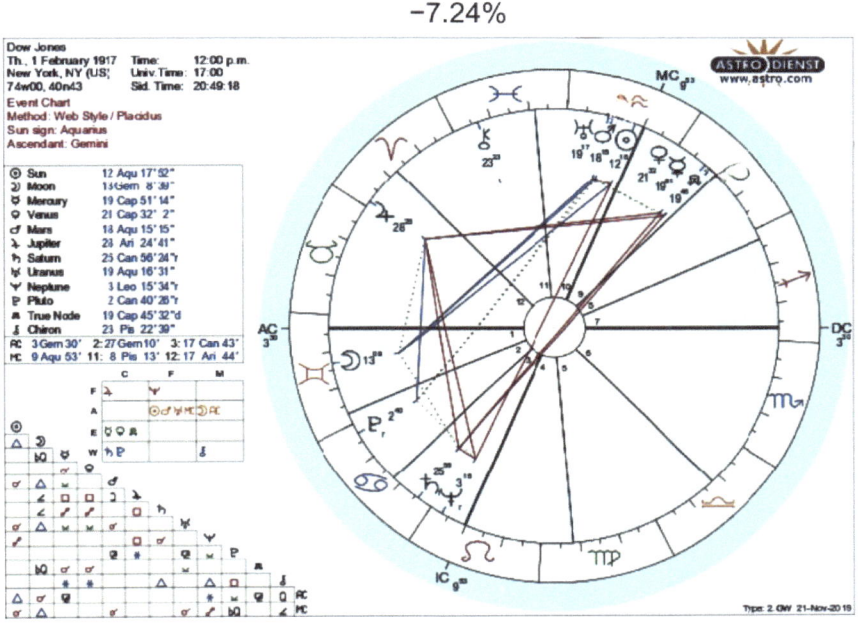

Here is where Mars was positioned in the sky on that day

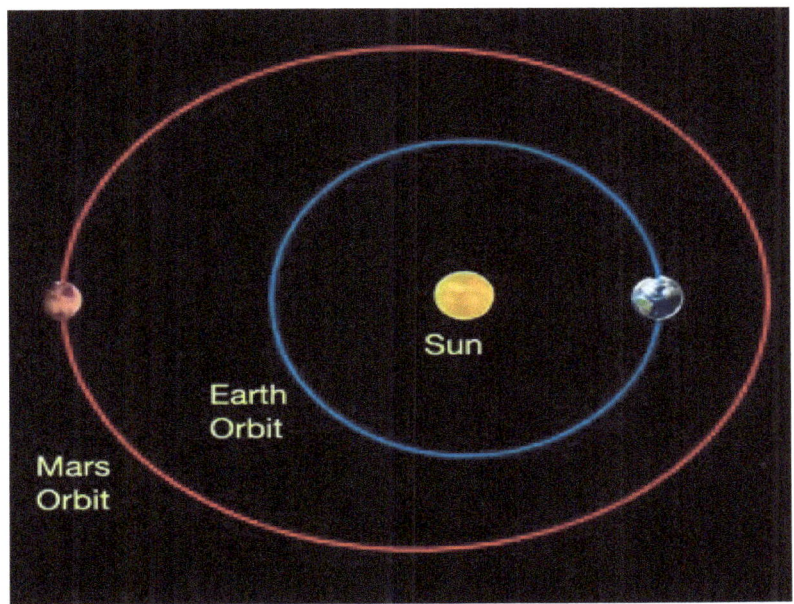

On October 27, 1997, the stock market crashed -7.18%

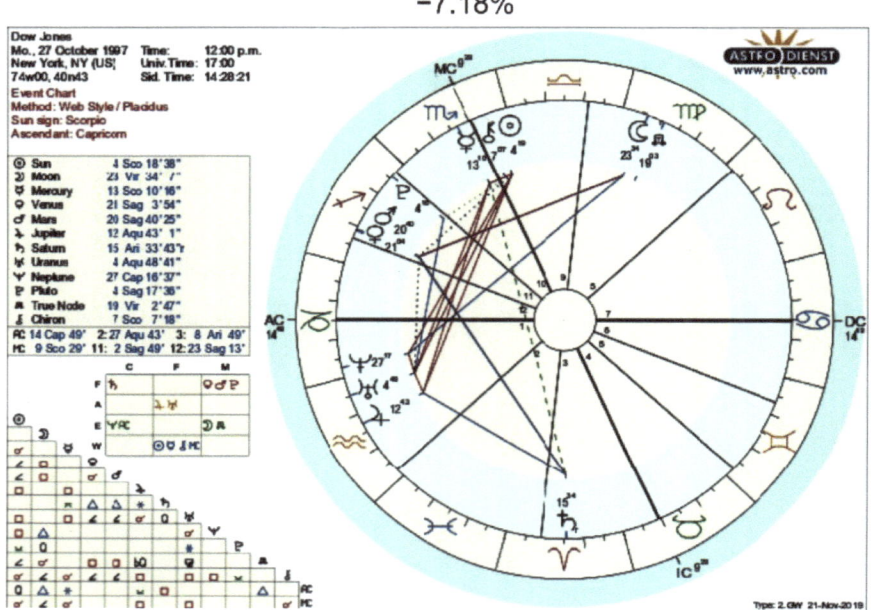

Here is where Mars was positioned in the sky on that day

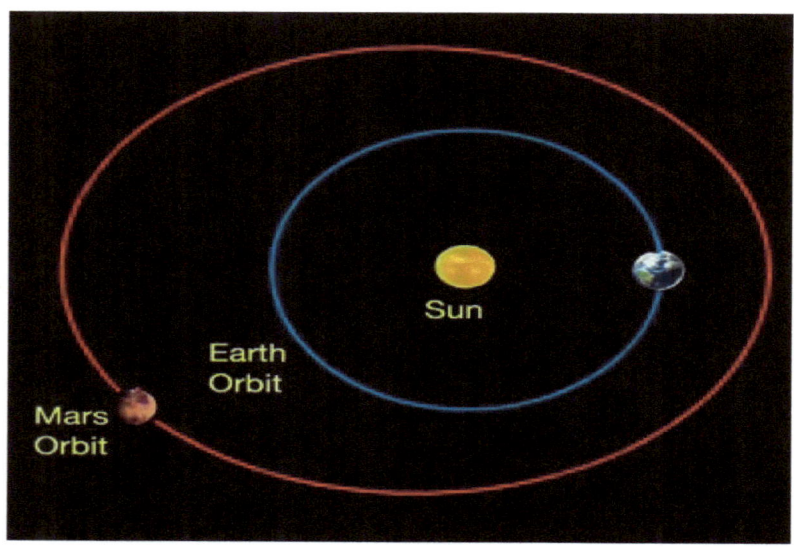

October 5, 1932, the stock market dropped -7.15 percent

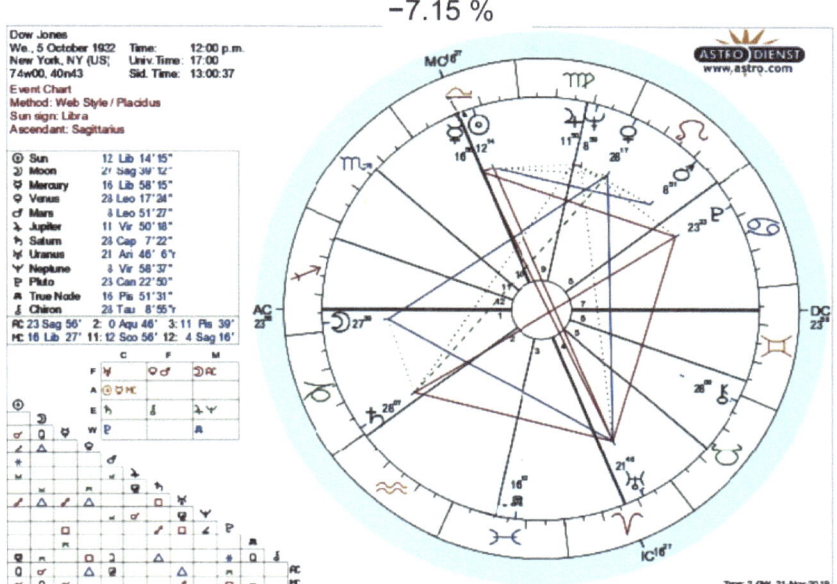

Here is where Mars was positioned in the sky on that day

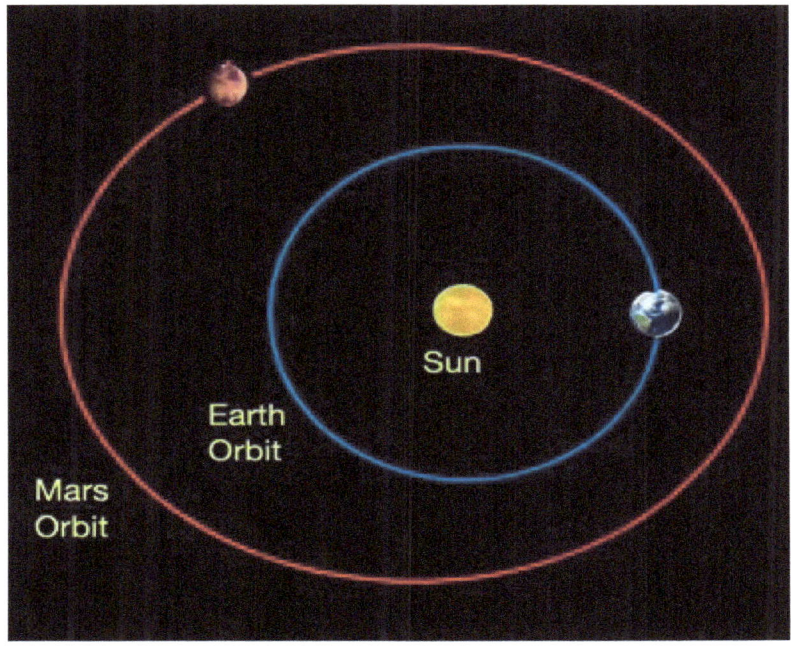

September 17, 2001, the stock market fell -7.13%

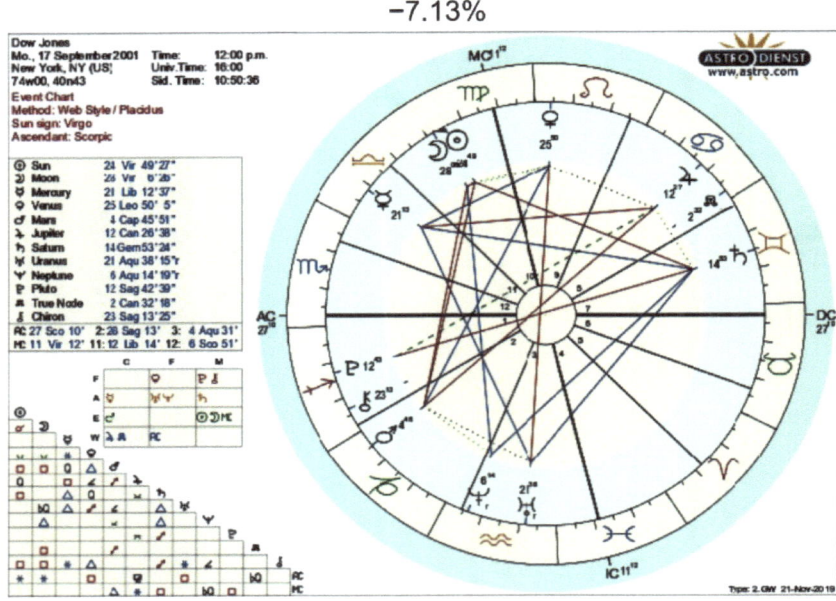

Here is where Mars was positioned in the sky that day

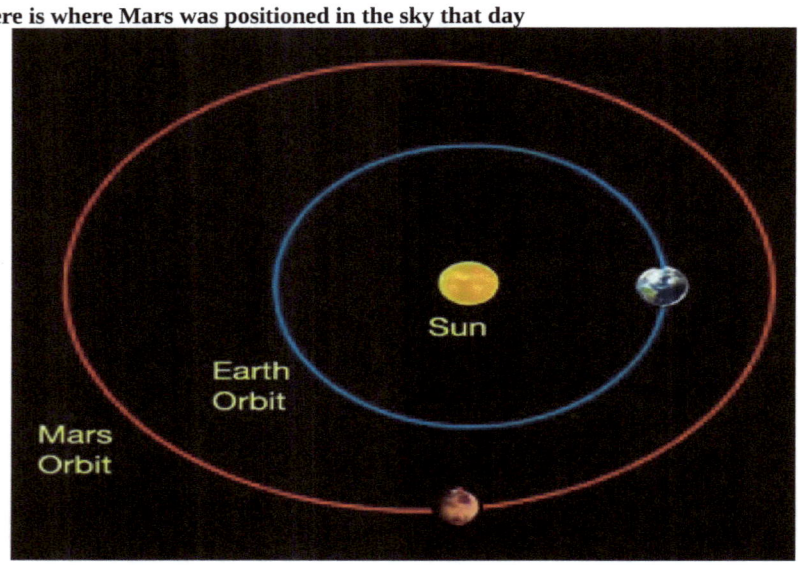

September 24, 1931, the stock market dropped -7.07%

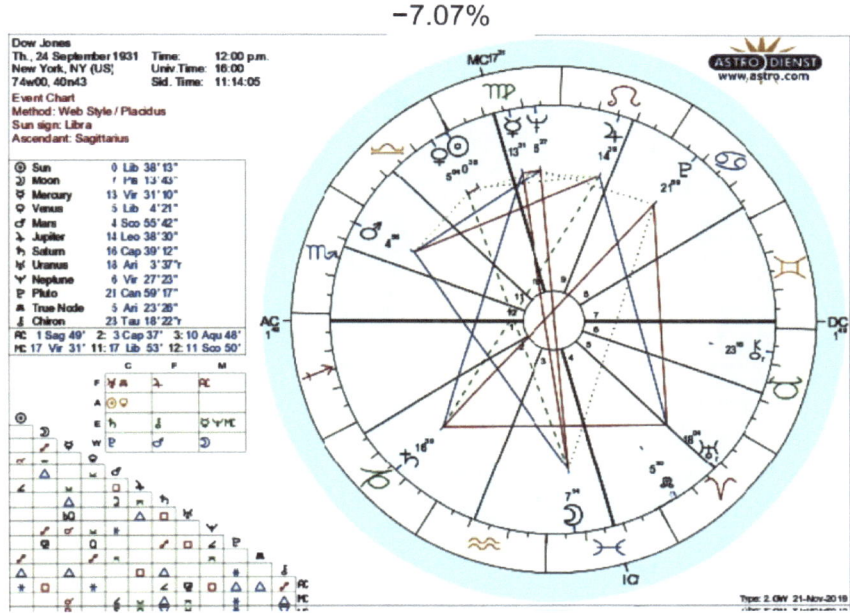

Here is where Mars was positioned in the sky on that day

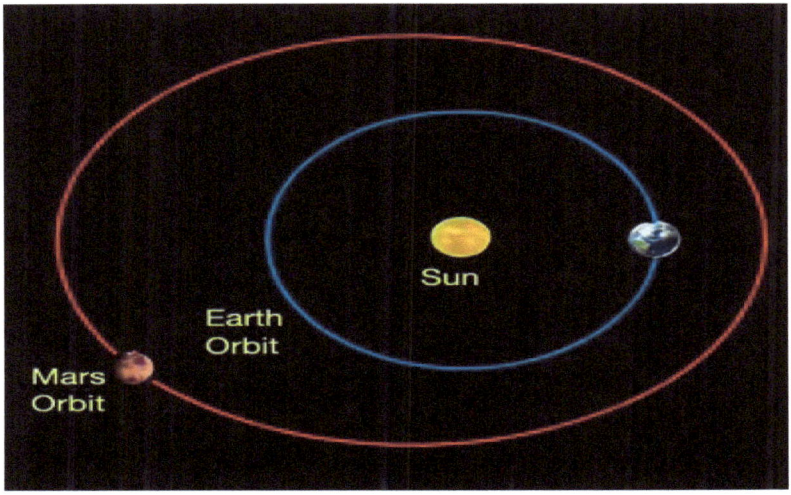

July 20, 1932, the stock market dropped -7.07%

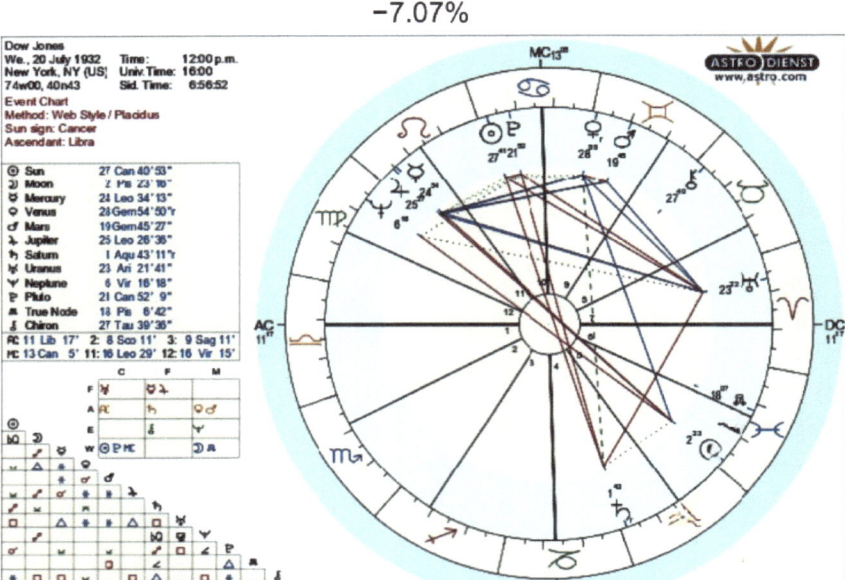

Here is where Mars was positioned in the sky that day

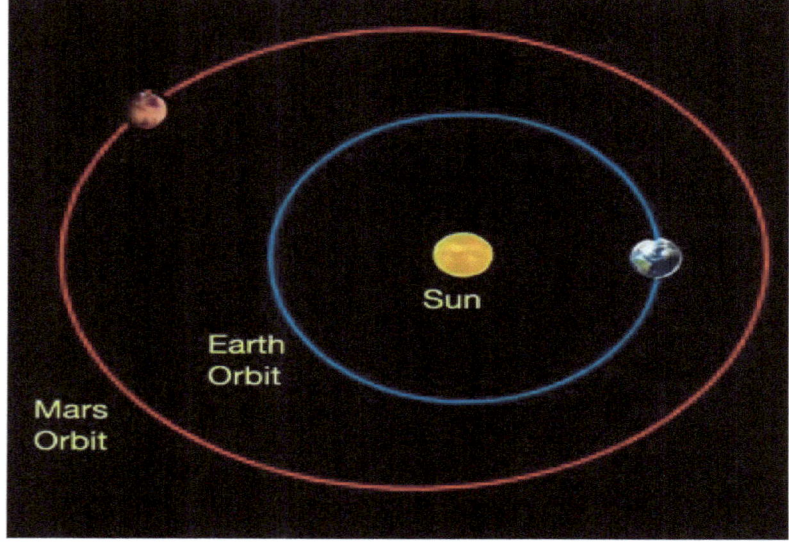

July 30, 1914, the stock market dropped -6.91%

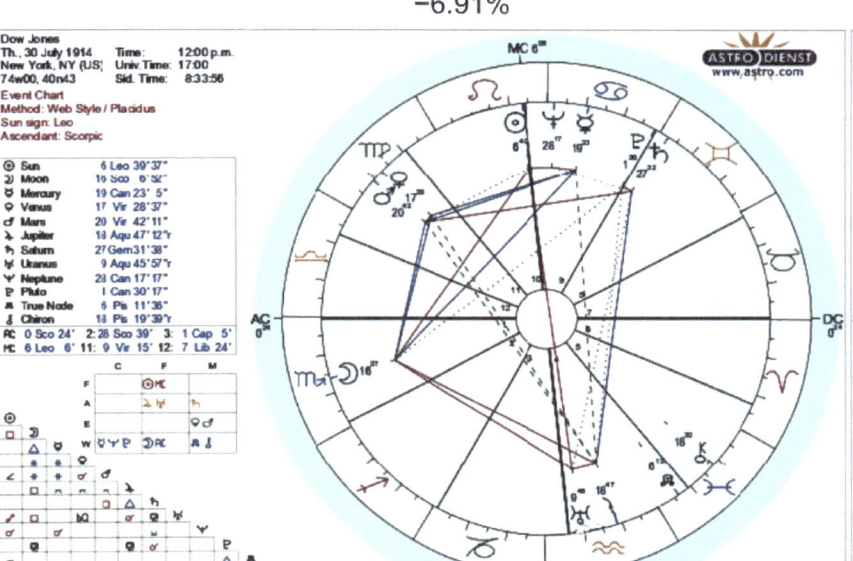

Here is where Mars was positioned in the sky on that day

September 29, 2008, the stock market dropped – 6.98%

-6.98%

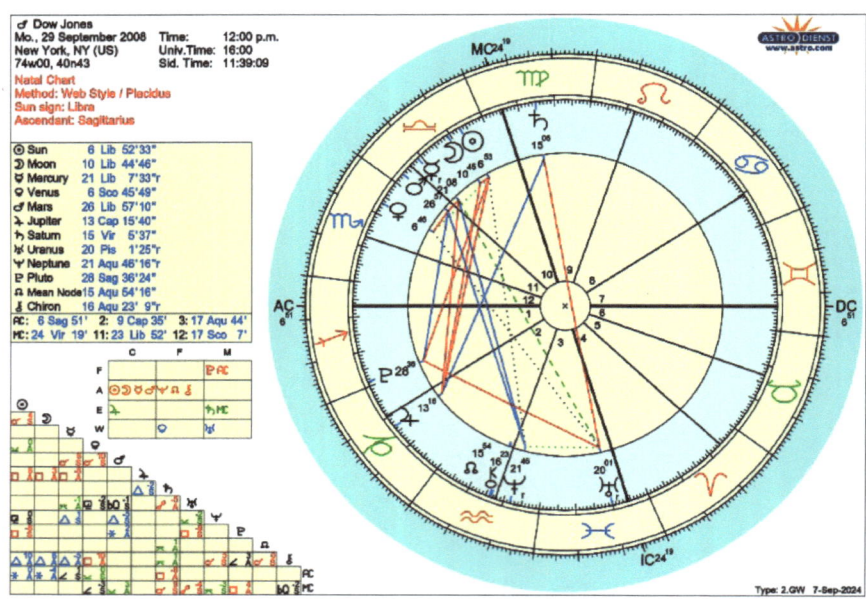

Here is where Mars was positioned in the sky that day

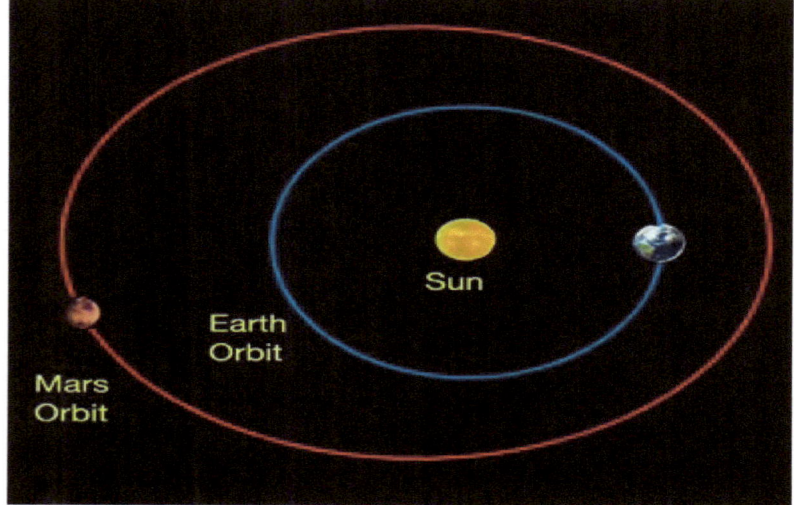

August 8, 2011, the stock market dropped -5.15%

-5.15%

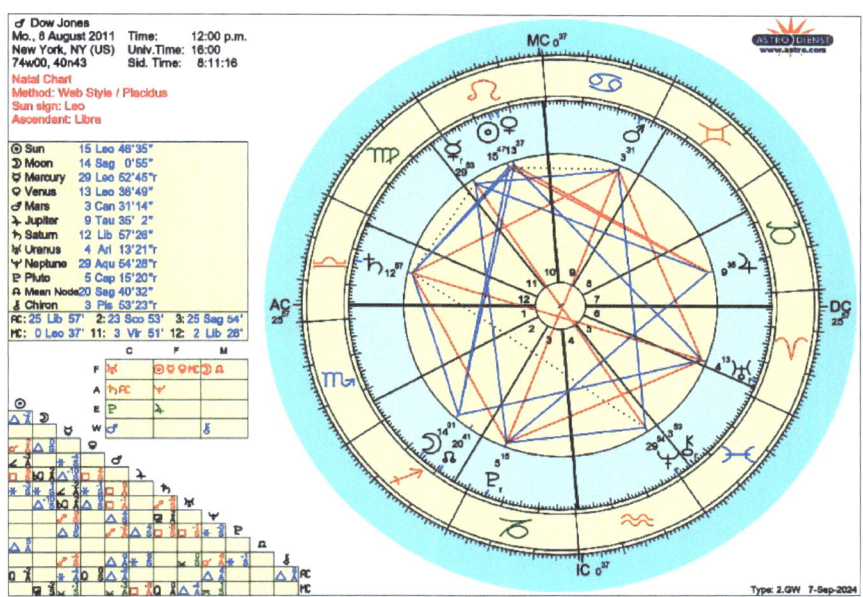

Here is where Mars was positioned in the sky on that day

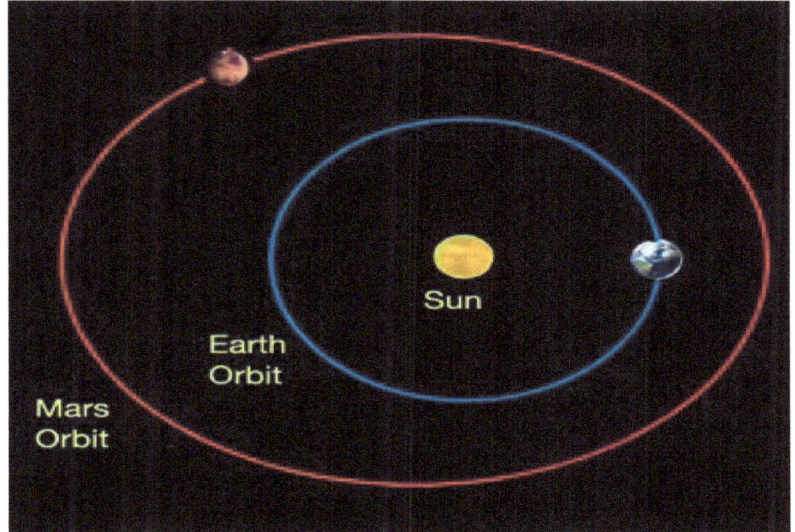

April 14, 2000, the stock market dropped -5.66%

-5.66%

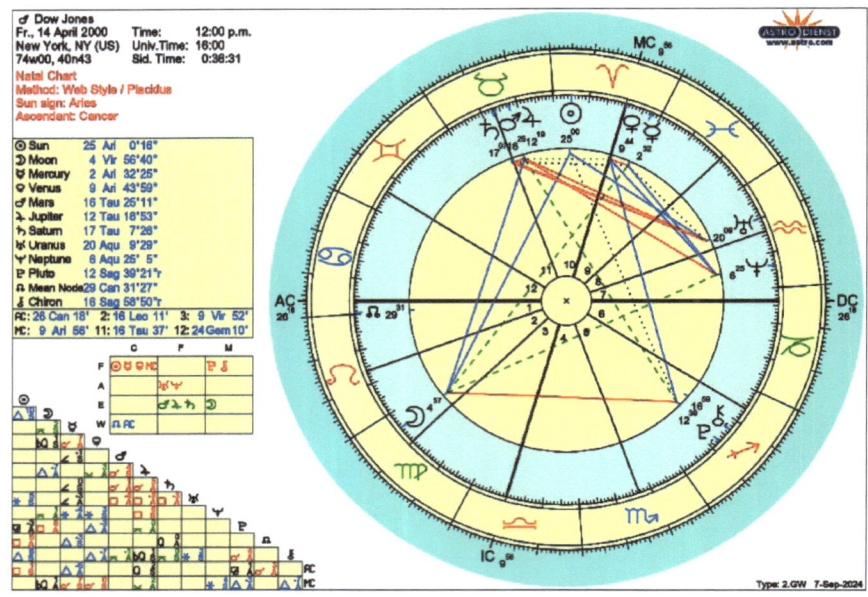

Here is where Mars was positioned in the sky that day

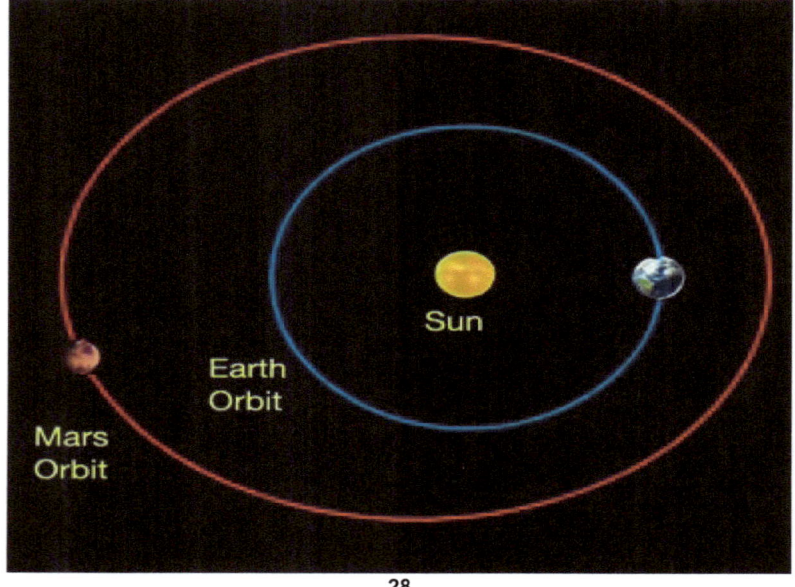

In all the days of major stock market crashes and downturns in the Dow Jones history, Mars was always in the orbital phase, from earth's point of view, marked with the white line.

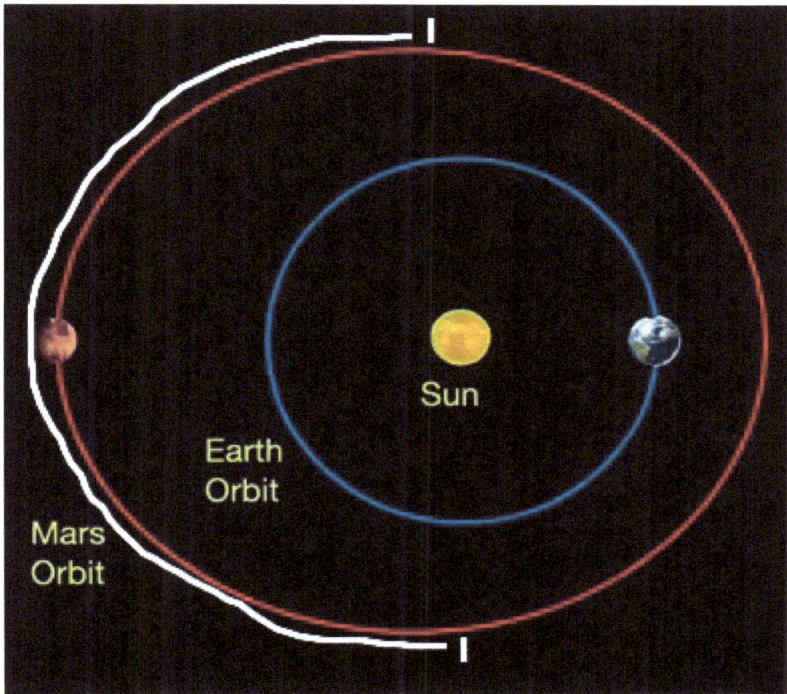

This data shows that a major stock market crash will never happen when Mars is orbiting in the area not marked with the white line. We can say this with 100% certainty.

The white area is the phase of the orbit when Mars is going further out from earth, but also when it's gravity is puling Earth's axial tilt towards the sun, possibly bringing warmer temperatures, which should affect investor sentiment most negatively, presuming that warmer temperatures relative to the mean affect cognitive function and trigger some variant of irritability or pessimism. There are studies that corroborate this dynamic between warmer temperatures and negative mood states.

Outside of the white area, as Mars gets closer to earth, Mars's gravity is puling earth's axial tilt away from the sun, bring presumably cooler temperatures, and less negative mood outcomes, which may explain why major stock market crashes never happen during that phase of Mars's orbit

Sources

The Dow's Biggest One-Day Drops

Here's where yesterday's drop of 586 points ranks among the worst drops in the Dow's history:

Date	Close	Change	Percent
9/29/2008	10,365.45	-777.68	-6.98%
10/15/2008	8,577.91	-733.08	-7.87%
9/17/2001	8,920.70	-684.81	-7.13%
12/1/2008	8,149.09	-679.95	-7.70%
10/9/2008	8,579.19	-678.92	-7.33%
8/8/2011	10,809.85	-634.76	-5.55%
4/14/2000	10,305.78	-617.78	-5.66%
8/24/2015	15,873.22	-586.53	-3.56%
10/27/1997	7,161.14	-554.26	-7.18%
8/21/2015	16,459.75	-530.94	-3.12%

Largest daily percentage losses[5]

Rank	Date	Close	Change Net	Change %
1	1987-10-19	1,738.74	-508.00	-22.61
2	2020-03-16	20,188.52	-2,997.10	-12.93
3	1929-10-28	260.64	-38.33	-12.82
4	1929-10-29	230.07	-30.57	-11.73
5	2020-03-12	21,200.62	-2,352.60	-9.99
6	1929-11-06	232.13	-25.55	-9.92
7	1899-12-18	58.27	-5.57	-8.72
8	1932-08-12	63.11	-5.79	-8.40
9	1907-03-14	76.23	-6.89	-8.29
10	1987-10-26	1,793.93	-156.83	-8.04
11	2008-10-15	8,577.91	-733.08	-7.87
12	1933-07-21	88.71	-7.55	-7.84
13	2020-03-09	23,851.02	-2,013.76	-7.79
14	1937-10-18	125.73	-10.57	-7.75
15	2008-12-01	8,149.09	-679.95	-7.70
16	2008-10-09	8,579.19	-678.91	-7.33
17	1917-02-01	88.52	-6.91	-7.24
18	1997-10-27	7,161.14	-554.26	-7.18
19	1932-10-05	66.07	-5.09	-7.15
20	2001-09-17	8,920.70	-684.81	-7.13

www.ingramcontent.com/pod-product-compliance
Lightning Source LLC
Chambersburg PA
CBHW040343220526
45473CB00009B/2776